THIS JOURNAL BELONGS TO

....

NOTE FROM THE AUTHOR

Everyone needs a hug! And as you delve into the pages of your Bible, using this Journal as a guide to embracing God, He will respond with His own arms opened wide. As you seek Him, you will find that He will draw you nearer to Himself in an ever more intimate relationship.

Years ago, I decided to follow Abraham's example and pursue God in a life of obedient faith, one step at a time. Knowing God better each day has become *The Magnificent Obsession* of my life. My relationship with God is developed daily as I read His Word, apply it to my life, then live it out on the anvil of my everyday experience.

This Journal is the result of my heartfelt desire to help you in your pursuit of a God-filled life. It is designed to keep you focused on Him through His Word, while encouraging you to record your own reflections and discoveries. Throughout the pages, I will share with you some of my own thoughts for your encouragement.

As you spend time with God each day, thoughtfully meditating on His Word and applying it to your life, you will increasingly experience a vibrant authenticity and practical relevancy to your faith that will be…

heart-stirring,

mind-expanding,

purpose-fulfilling,

life-stretching!

You will get to know God as Abraham did…as His friend. So turn the page…and begin now to enjoy *His* embrace.

Anne Graham Lotz

Founder and president of AnGeL Ministries, Anne Graham Lotz has shared her heart for God with people on all seven continents. The daughter of Billy and Ruth Bell Graham, she proclaims the Word of God in towns and cities around the world. *Embracing God* is excerpted from her book *The Magnificent Obsession*. To find out more, check out www.annegrahamlotz.com.

EMBRACING
GOD
JOURNAL

ANNE
GRAHAM
LOTZ

Ellie
Claire
gift & paper expressions

...inspired by life

A Deeper Journey

How can you use this journal to get the most out of your faith journey?
There are several ways. Interact with the text. Read the Bible verses and
study them in context from your Bible. Or simply read each entry and
ask yourself these questions:

- *What spiritual lesson is God conveying through this entry/verse?*
- *How does this lesson apply to my life?*
- *What response is God asking of me today to embrace Him to the fullest?*

By recording your answers in the lined section, you will have an account of
your personal faith journey that you can go back to again and again.

. . . .

. . . .

. . . .

. . . .

. . . .

. . . .

. . . .

. . . .

. . . .

. . . .

. . . .

. . . .

. . . .

. . . .

. . . .

. . . .

. . . .

. . . .

. . . .

. . . .

I want to know God as Abraham did...as His friend. As His friend.
The Bible reveals an astonishing fact when it describes Abraham as God's friend.
The designation "friend" comes from God's perspective.

LEAVE EVERYTHING BEHIND

They sought God eagerly, and he was found by them.

2 CHRONICLES 15:15

*D*eep down, in the secret recesses of my soul, I long to know
God in spirit and in truth. I yearn for God to fill my life,
saturating me with Himself.

But how does a person today even begin to pursue knowing God?
How does someone even take the first step in God's direction?

For me, the process began with a small desire in my heart,
a small thought in my mind, a small light in my eye,
a small turning of my spirit when I observed the example of
someone else who pursued God. Nothing really big and flashy.

Do you want to know God? Could Abraham serve as the example
for all of us? Has the magnificent obsession begun in your heart
and mind and eye and spirit? Maybe the small spark of desire
has been fanned into flame by what you have observed in the
created world around you or by your conscience within you.
I do know that if you and I ever truly know God, it will not be
an accident. It will be because we have pursued with focused
intentionality. It will happen when, like Abraham, we abandon
every other goal, every other priority, and embrace the
God-filled life until He becomes our magnificent obsession.

*H*e doesn't show up *only* when He parts the Red Sea with a powerful wind, or in the banquet hall with handwriting on the wall, or on Mount Sinai with thunder and lightning, or on the Mount of Transfiguration in radiant glory. He shows up in everyday situations, as we are going about our everyday responsibilities in our everyday routines.

When they saw the courage of Peter and John and realized that they
were unschooled, ordinary men, they were astonished and they
took note that these men had been with Jesus.

ACTS 4:13

If you want to truly know God in a vibrant, personal relationship, then you must leave everything behind, including that which is familiar, the places of fence-sitting compromise, and your fear of living a life that will be very different from the people around you.

*In the same way, any of you who does not give up
everything he has cannot be my disciple.*

Could it be that you have made the choice to leave everything behind, then followed through with the commitment to let everything go in order to pursue knowing God...and now you're wondering, What in the world have I done? God knows where you are.

"*For I know the plans I have for you,*" *declares the LORD,* "*plans to prosper you and not to harm you, plans to give you hope and a future.*"

JEREMIAH 29:11

The best way for you and me to overcome our fear of those people so unlike us who surround us in our everyday lives is to keep our focus on the Lord and cultivate an awareness of His presence in our lives. We need to learn to be more aware of *Him* than of *them*.

*You will keep in perfect peace him whose mind is steadfast,
because he trusts in you.*

ISAIAH 26:3

When God called him out of his familiar place, Abraham leaped to obey, making the choice to take steps that began a journey that lasted a lifetime. Abraham's willingness to leave everything behind arrested me, challenged me, convicted me. Would I be willing to do the same? Could I ever really know God if I didn't choose to leave everything behind?

Be strong and courageous. Do not be afraid or terrified...for the LORD your God goes with you; he will never leave you nor forsake you.

DEUTERONOMY 31:6

It doesn't matter if you can't remember how or when or where you began to wander. Are you hesitating because you feel ashamed and embarrassed? Because you are not sure God will receive you? He will. So…don't keep Him waiting. Leave everything behind…the familiar, the fence sitting, the fear, the failure…and run back to Him!

ake words with you and return to the LORD. Say to him: "Forgive all our sins and receive us graciously, that we may offer the fruit of our lips."

HOSEA 14:2

LET EVERYTHING GO

One thing I do, forgetting those things which are behind and reaching forward to those things which are ahead, I press toward the goal for the prize of the upward call of God in Christ Jesus.

PHILIPPIANS 3:13–14 NKJV

*U*nless and until you and I are willing to let everything go, including our old friends, we will never discover the friends God wants to give us and the blessings He wants to pour out on us. And who knows? If we let everything go and embrace the magnificent obsession, maybe at least some of our friends will be so intrigued that they will embrace it too.

What's keeping you from pursuing the magnificent obsession? By reading this journal and sharing my goal, you're saying you want to know God as Abraham did. You're saying you want to receive the fullness of His blessing. You're saying you want to be a blessing. You're saying you want to fulfill the potential He has for your life. You're saying you are embracing the God-filled life. You're saying you want everything He has to give you. But…what's that I see clutched in your hand? If you insist on getting what you want, on what you have a right to have, watch out! You may get it! And you may then wind up with a lot less than God wants you to give you. Don't miss out! Let it go! Let it go!

LET EVERYTHING GO!

*S*ometimes the solution to a problem is just to give up and let go of your right to be right, your right to an inheritance, your right to special attention, your right to go first, your right to a certain seat, or to a certain place, or to a certain privilege, or to a certain position. Just give it up. Let it go. Don't let selfishness keep you from solving the problem and restoring peace.

*Therefore, since we are surrounded by such a great cloud of witnesses,
let us throw off everything that hinders and the sin that so easily entangles,
and let us run with perseverance the race marked out for us.*

HEBREWS 12:1

From personal experience, I know that my prayer life tends to be very shallow unless I deliberately, intentionally make the effort to deepen and develop it on a daily basis. Prayer was central to Abraham's life. What a simple, fundamental principle that is as necessary today as it was then. In fact, prayer must be central to our lives if we are serious about embracing the magnificent obsession. So...how's *your* prayer life?

....

....

....

....

....

....

....

....

....

....

....

....

....

*s [Jesus] was praying, heaven was opened and
the Holy Spirit descended on him.*

LUKE 3:21-22

If we want our families to be saved from the judgment that is coming, then letting go of everything is not an option. Do not despise God's gracious offer of salvation by clinging to our own prejudices and perspective and pride and possessions and position. Just let it go.

But seek first his kingdom and his righteousness,
and all these things will be given to you as well.

MATTHEW 6:33

*W*ho is watching *you* and the way you handle your problems and disputes? Often it's someone you don't even know is watching. But you and I can count on the fact that one reason God allows us to have problems is so we can demonstrate to a watching world how His children respond.

In this you greatly rejoice, though now for a little while you may have had to suffer grief in all kinds of trials. These have come so that your faith— of greater worth than gold, which perishes even though refined by fire— may be proved genuine and may result in praise, glory and honor when Jesus Christ is revealed.

1 PETER 1:6–7

Abraham had let everything go, including first choice of the land God had promised to give him. He impressed me as someone who wanted to be right with God more than he wanted to insist on his own rights. He wanted to maintain his testimony more than he wanted to accumulate the world's treasures. He wanted peace in his home more than he wanted property and possessions. And, so he had to just let everything go.

*Whoever tries to keep his life will lose it,
and whoever loses his life will preserve it.*

LUKE 17:33

I learned that you can't outgive God. If I just give up and let go, what He gives me in return makes what I had clenched in my fist seem so small and worthless.

God is able to make all grace abound to you, so that in all things at all times, having all that you need, you will abound in every good work.

2 CORINTHIANS 9:8

ENTRUST EVERYTHING COMPLETELY

And without faith it is impossible to please God, because anyone who comes to him must believe that he exists and that he rewards those who earnestly seek him.

One day an acrobat staged a dramatic performance by walking on a tightrope across Niagara Falls. He took a wheelbarrow and pushed it over the tightrope. When he turned and came back, this time the applause was thunderous. But when he picked up a burlap bag of sand, placed it in the wheelbarrow, and began to push it across the tightrope...the crowd gasped, then burst into applause.

The acrobat bowed dramatically to the crowd, then issued a challenge: "I'd like to do something even more spectacular!" he said. "But first let me ask you something: since the bag of sand weighs the same as an average-size man, how many of you believe I can take a man across the tightrope in a wheelbarrow?"

"We believe you can do that. You can do it!" everyone shouted.

Then the acrobat asked, "All right, which one of you will be that man?" A shriveled little old man in the back raised his hand as he stepped forward. "I've seen what you've done, and I've heard what you've said. I believe you can push me across, so I'll do it."

He climbed into the wheelbarrow, and the acrobat set out across the tightrope. On the final return, the roar of the crowd was deafening. The acrobat gallantly bowed, saluted, smiled broadly, and said, "Thank you, sir, for really believing in me."

Everyone in the crowd at Niagara Falls *said* they believed in the acrobat, but only the old man demonstrated genuine faith.

What thrilling reassurance to know that Abraham's God, and Isaiah's God, is also *my* God. And He speaks personally to you and me too.

....

....

....

....

....

....

....

....

....

....

....

....

....

....

....

This is what the Lord says—
he who created you, O Jacob,
he who formed you, O Israel:
"Fear not, for I have redeemed you;
I have summoned you by name; you are mine."

ISAIAH 43:1

$\mathcal{G}$od's Word comes to you and me clearly when we read our Bibles. When you are confused about what God is saying to you, open your Bible and listen as you read.

_Above all, you must understand that no prophecy of Scripture
came about by the prophet's own interpretation. For prophecy never
had its origin in the will of man, but men spoke from God as they
were carried along by the Holy Spirit._

2 PETER 1:20–21

One of the most amazing, mind-blowing, thrilling aspects of hearing the voice of the Lord speak to me through His Word is that when He does, He reveals that He not only knows what's going on in my life but He also understands what's going on inside of me. He understands my fears.

....

....

....

....

....

....

....

....

....

....

....

....

....

....

....

_____
_____
_____
_____
_____
_____
_____
_____
_____
_____
_____
_____
_____
_____
_____

You know when I sit and when I rise;
you perceive my thoughts from afar.
Before a word is on my tongue
you know it completely, O LORD.

PSALM 139:2, 4

*H*ave you ever been plagued by the what-ifs? What has given you panic attacks? Why does your stomach turn over and your face drain of color and your heart race at just the thought of whatever it is? What secret fears are lurking in the deep recesses of your heart?

....

....

....

....

....

....

....

....

....

....

....

....

....

....

....

Do not be afraid, Abram.
I am your shield,
your very great reward.

GENESIS 15:1

How often I've found that my lack of peace is directly related to my lack of Bible reading. If *you* lack peace, if you are afraid, could it be that you are neglecting to read your Bible or diminishing its importance? The psalmist testified, "Great peace have they who love your law." God will give you and me promises that bring peace in the midst of our panic, but we must tune our hearts to listen to His voice.

....

....

....

....

....

....

....

....

....

....

....

....

....

....

....

Do not be anxious about anything, but in everything, by prayer and petition, with thanksgiving, present your requests to God. And the peace of God, which transcends all understanding, will guard your hearts and your minds in Christ Jesus.

PHILIPPIANS 4:6–7

*P*raise God! He understands me! He draws near to me! And in the midst of my secret loneliness, His Word gives me an awareness of His presence in my life, just as He did for Abraham.

Have I not commanded you? Be strong and courageous. Do not be terrified; do not be discouraged, for the LORD your God will be with you wherever you go.

JOSHUA 1:9

At the cross, God swore by Himself that He's committed to you. There is nothing you will ever do, nothing you will ever fail to do, nothing you could ever do, nothing you could ever fail to do.... There is nothing that can or will ever, *ever, EVER* break the covenant. You didn't do anything to earn it, and you can't do anything to lose it. All you have to do is receive it by trusting everything completely to Him.

He who did not spare his own Son, but gave him up for us all—
how will he not also, along with him, graciously give us all things?

ROMANS 8:32

PURSUE EVERYTHING PATIENTLY

I waited patiently for the LORD;
he turned to me and heard my cry.

PSALM 40:1

Sometimes it can be very hard for us to wait on God to do things in His time and in His way. It doesn't occur to us that He has intentionally delayed answering our prayer or fulfilling His promise because He has a higher, greater purpose in mind than just giving us what we want, when we want it, the way we want it. Delay doesn't necessarily mean denial. It's just that God often uses the delay to develop our faith in Him as we struggle to patiently pursue everything He has for us.

God sometimes seems to be *soooooo* slow! And we can become so impatient that we run ahead of Him, thinking we can either help Him answer our prayer or force Him to act on our timetable. If we don't learn to walk alongside Him at His pace, we end up making a mess. We may become entangled in consequences that bind and complicate our own lives and damage the lives of others to an almost unbearable degree.

When you pray, have you used your imagination to tell God how to fulfill His promise and answer your desperate plea? Instead of waiting on Him, are you running ahead by manipulating what He has said to fit into your timetable or desires? Since you know what He has promised, do you feel you are justified in helping Him out?

....

....

....

....

....

....

....

....

....

....

....

....

....

....

But if we hope for what we do not yet have,
we wait for it patiently.

ROMANS 8:25

If you seek God's guidance with an open mind, humbly willing to do whatever He says, He will teach you the right way to go and "land" you safely in the center of His will. That's His promise.

....

....

....

....

....

....

....

....

....

....

....

....

....

....

....

....

*He guides the humble in what is right
and teaches them his way.*

PSALM 25:9

Running away never really solves anything. It just delays dealing with whatever or whomever you are running from. But no matter where you are, no matter how far you've run, remember this: God is so good!

"Can anyone hide in secret places so that I cannot see him?"
declares the LORD. "Do not I fill heaven and earth?"

JEREMIAH 23:24

When have you talked to the Lord about where you've been and where you're going, about what you're doing and who you belong to, about how you're feeling? God already knows all the answers. He just wants you to talk things over with Him. Have you?

[Hagar] gave this name to the LORD who spoke to her:
"You are the God who sees me."

GENESIS 16:13

Have you ever had an attack of the if-onlys? They can send you into a downward spiral of depression as they seem to extend way, way back in your life, can't they? I've had to take all of those painful regrets to the foot of the cross and leave them there, lay myself down in God's grace, and plead for His mercy to break the emotional and spiritual paralysis *if-onlys* can cause.

....

....

....

....

....

....

....

....

....

....

....

....

....

....

*Have mercy on me, O God,
according to your unfailing love;
according to your great compassion
blot out my transgressions.
Wash away all my iniquity
and cleanse me from my sin.*

PSALM 51:1–2

*Be encouraged! Praise God! He is the God of second chances...
and third...and fourth.*

*You are forgiving and good, O Lord, abounding
in love to all who call to you.*

PSALM 86:5

Are you afraid to refocus on God's face after failure because you think you will "see" anger or disdain or condemnation or rejection or indifference? Then look again! God loves you! He wants you to know Him, and He is sufficient for your every need.

....

....

....

....

....

....

....

....

....

....

....

....

....

....

....

....

....

....

....

....

....

....

This is love: not that we loved God, but that he loved us and sent his Son as an atoning sacrifice for our sins.

1 JOHN 4:10

LIFT EVERYTHING UP

Evening, and morning, and at noon, will I pray,
and cry aloud: and he shall hear my voice.

PSALM 55:17 KJV

*P*rayer must be central to our lives if we are serious about embracing the magnificent obsession.

Prayer has always been a struggle for me. In fact, I've described it is as the fight of my life. If there is anything consistent about it, it's that I consistently struggle to maintain a quality time alone with God every day. I fail more often than I succeed.
I have become more determined to learn how to really pray.
I'm not interested in fancy rhetoric, or eloquent oratory, or endless monologues, or mystical languages.

I don't want to engage in hyperventilating, chair-jumping, room-rocking, head-banging, or aisle-dancing theatrics.

And I don't want to adopt one of the religious mantra-chanting, bead-counting, incense-burning, rag-tying rituals.

I just want to talk to God.

I want to talk to Him...but not do all the talking.

I want to know that He is listening.

I want to hear what He says back to me...and understand what He means by what He says.

I want my prayers to be like reversed thunder.

When I pray, I want to get heaven's attention.

I want my prayers to be clear, completely understood two-way conversations with God, the kind of communication Abraham had with Him.

Walking with God is like walking with a friend. If we want to walk with Him, we must walk in His direction, which means we must surrender the will of our life to Him. We can't go off in our own direction, deciding our own goals and pursuing our own purposes. And we must walk at His pace, which means step-by-step obedience to His Word.

*Dear friends, let us love one another, for love comes from God.
Everyone who loves has been born of God and knows God. Whoever
does not love does not know God, because God is love.*

1 John 4:7-8

One thing I have discovered is that God won't adjust His pace or direction to suit me. I have to adjust my pace and direction to His if I want to walk with Him. How is your walk? Are you walking at His pace and in His direction? What will you have to leave, from whom will you have to slip away, where will you have to go in order to make time each day to adjust your pace and direction to God's?

_____

_____

_____

_____

_____

_____

_____

_____

_____

_____

_____

_____

_____

_____

_____

_____

_____

_____

_____

What does the LORD your God ask of you but to fear the LORD your God, to walk in all his ways, to love him, to serve the LORD your God with all your heart and with all your soul.

DEUTERONOMY 10:12

God reveals what's on His mind to those who make the time to walk with Him as a friend.

I no longer call you servants, because a servant does not know his master's business. Instead, I have called you friends, for everything that I learned from my Father I have made known to you.

God's Word is like our schoolmaster, teaching us God's perspective and God's principles, God's wisdom and God's way, God's standards and God's truth, God's viewpoint and God's values. Without God's Word, we're just guessing.

The law was our schoolmaster to bring us unto Christ,
that we might be justified by faith.

GALATIANS 3:24 KJV

I wonder...what blessings have I missed because I haven't made the time to stay in His presence? Has God wanted to reveal Himself to me in a way I've never seen before, but I've been in such a hurry I didn't have time to linger? Do you rush through your time with God too? Let's slow down... let's keep our eyes closed and our heads bowed for just a few minutes longer. Let's reflect on the day's Scripture reading for just one more moment.

Come near to God and he will come near to you.

JAMES 4:8

*D*o you believe that God actually exists exactly as He is revealed in Scripture? When you pray, are you confident that you are speaking to a living, invisible Person?

....

....

....

....

....

....

....

....

....

....

....

....

....

....

....

....

....

....

....

....

....

*ow faith is being sure of what we hope for
and certain of what we do not see.*

*S*ometimes, when we don't know what to pray, it helps to just start praying. God can direct us more specifically as we pray.

_____

_____

_____

_____

_____

_____

_____

_____

_____

_____

_____

_____

_____

_____

_____

[Gabriel] instructed me and said to me, "Daniel, I have now come to give you insight and understanding. As soon as you began to pray, an answer was given, which I have come to tell you, for you are highly esteemed."

DANIEL 9:22–23

CAST EVERYTHING OUT

This is what God the LORD says—
he who created the heavens and stretched them out,
who spread out the earth and all that comes out of it...
"I, the LORD, have called you in righteousness;
I will take hold of your hand."

ISAIAH 42:5–6

God is so gracious to sinners, even those of us who are repeat
offenders. There have been times when I knew I deserved
God's punishment for my attitude or my actions or my words.
Several years ago, I found myself wrestling with a sin which has
been a source of struggle and frustration for most of my life. Faced
with my repeated failure, I crawled back in humiliation to the foot
of the cross, where I expected to hear God tick off, one by one,
the dire consequences of my sin or, at the very least, to hear Him
sternly rebuke me. Instead, God affirmed His love for me and His
promise of blessing and His call upon my life. My heart melted!
I got up off my knees and, instead of quitting, I passionately
recommitted myself to Him. I learned once again, from firsthand
experience, that "a bruised reed he will not break, and a smoldering
wick he will not snuff out."

As I have grown in my knowledge of God's Word and matured
in my faith and walked more closely with the Lord, I have been
faced with a very unpleasant surprise: my conflict with sin has not
lessened; it has intensified! In response I have had only two real
options: I could decide I can't get past this conflict, quit, and just
be grateful I'm going to heaven when I die, *or*, by God's grace and
in His power, I could break the cycle of sin!

Are you spiritually weak because your prayers seem to be unanswered and you are tempted to doubt God has heard and will answer you? Have you taken your eyes off the Lord and placed them on your circumstances?

Against all hope, Abraham in hope believed and so became the father of many nations, just as it had been said to him, "So shall your offspring be."

ROMANS 4:18

When Jesus comes to live within us, there is such joy! Then our hearts are flooded with peace, our days are filled with purpose, our eyes are focused upward, our spirits bask in His unconditional love, our souls rest in His grace. And our life in Christ is more than wonderful.

*Thou wilt shew me the path of life: in thy presence is fulness of joy;
at thy right hand there are pleasures for evermore.*

PSALM 16:11 KJV

It's so hard to acknowledge that, on my own, I have no power to be good in God's sight.

I know that nothing good lives in me, that is, in my sinful nature. For I have the desire to do what is good, but I cannot carry it out. For what I do is not the good I want to do; no, the evil I do not want to do—this I keep on doing.

ROMANS 7:18-19

*H*ow can we possibly put to death our old nature inside us? I can testify from personal experience your old nature will die slowly and over time. But you *can* conquer it...one choice at a time, dozens of times a day, every day for the rest of your life.

....

....

....

....

....

....

....

....

....

....

....

....

....

....

....

You must rid yourselves of all such things as these: anger, rage, malice, slander, and filthy language from your lips. Do not lie to each other, since you have taken off your old self with its practices and have put on the new self, which is being renewed in knowledge in the image of its Creator.

*C*hoices. Sometimes the small, irritating ones are the hardest of all to make. But actually, if we make the choice, the indwelling Holy Spirit of God supernaturally gives us the power to carry it out.

When I want to do good, evil is right there with me.... Who will rescue me from this body of death? Thanks be to God—through Jesus Christ our Lord!

ROMANS 7:21, 24-25

Choices add up. God has given you His Spirit so that you have the power to make the right choices. As you do, and as your new nature grows, you will instinctively react and respond in the Spirit.

*Those controlled by the sinful nature cannot please God.
You, however, are controlled not by the sinful nature
but by the Spirit, if the Spirit of God lives in you.*

ROMANS 8:8–9

*W*hat happens at the judgment seat of Christ *then* is determined by our choices *now*. Praise God! We're not there yet. There is still time!

If any man builds on this foundation using gold, silver, costly stones, wood, hay or straw, his work will be shown for what it is, because the Day will bring it to light. It will be revealed with fire, and the fire will test the quality of each man's work. If what he has built survives, he will receive his reward.

1 CORINTHIANS 3:12–14

Lay Everything Down

*I have been crucified with Christ and I no longer live,
but Christ lives in me. The life I live in the body, I live by faith
in the Son of God, who loved me and gave himself for me.*

GALATIANS 2:20

In Abraham's pursuit to know God as his friend, he came to the supreme test of his devotion: whether or not he was willing to lay down not his own life but his most precious possession.

What is your most precious possession? Whatever it may be, to be God's friend, to receive all that He has for you, to experience the God-filled life, you must lay it down. Abraham must have thought he had laid down everything when he gave up Ishmael. But then, about ten years after that critical decision and decisive action to cast everything out, "God tested Abraham" (Genesis 22:1).

Satan tempts you and me to weaken us and draw out the sin in our lives, but God's purpose in testing us is to strengthen our faith and draw out the good.

Be prepared, because God will test you too. God tests us, but He always measures the test in proportion to our faith.

I've discovered that God knows exactly when and how to test me. But He has reassured me He will never give me a test or temptation greater than I can bear, although He does give me tests that I *think* are greater than I can bear—which is what makes them a test.

For me, one of the most thrilling blessings of knowing God is that He calls me by my name. *He knows me.* And He speaks to me personally through His Word.

....

....

....

....

....

....

....

....

....

....

....

....

....

....

....

You have said, "I know you by name and you have found favor with me."
If you are pleased with me, teach me your ways so
I may know you and continue to find favor with you.

EXODUS 33:12-13

*P*raise God! He speaks to me...and you...and Abraham...personally, in the language of our lives at any given moment in time. But we have to be available and willing to hear what He has to say. I wonder, how available are you to hear God's voice?

....

....

....

....

....

....

....

....

....

....

....

....

....

....

Obey my voice, and I will be your God, and ye shall be my people: and walk ye in all the ways that I have commanded you, that it may be well unto you.

JEREMIAH 7:23 KJV

I too have discovered that God is not always easy to listen to. Sometimes He convicts me of sin. Sometimes He forbids me to indulge in a favorite pastime. Sometimes He calls me to step out of my comfort zone and onto the surface of the stormy sea. Sometimes He commands me to do something I don't really want to do. What has He said to you that was hard to hear?

....

....

....

....

....

....

....

....

....

....

....

....

....

....

If only you had paid attention to my commands, your peace would have been like a river, your righteousness like the waves of the sea.

ISAIAH 48:18

I have found that once I make the decision to obey God's command, whatever it is, peace floods my heart.

Peace I leave with you; my peace I give you. I do not give to you as the world gives. Do not let your hearts be troubled and do not be afraid.

JOHN 14:27

One of the primary tactics of the enemy is to tempt you and me to doubt God's Word and to doubt God's character. What do you know of God from your experience? Make your own list. Use the experiences as stepping-stones in your walk of obedient faith.

....

....

....

....

....

....

....

....

....

....

....

....

....

....

I do believe; help me overcome my unbelief!

MARK 9:24

Are you so focused on what you must lay down you have lost focus on God's person and God's promises and God's power? Are you so focused on the cross and the tomb you are blinded to the resurrection and the crown? Would you take a moment to refocus? God is good. His promises are true. And His power is limitless.

....

....

....

....

....

....

....

....

....

....

....

....

....

Let us fix our eyes on Jesus, the author and perfecter of our faith, who for the joy set before him endured the cross, scorning its shame, and sat down at the right hand of the throne of God. Consider him who endured such opposition from sinful men, so that you will not grow weary and lose heart.

HEBREWS 12:2–3

As I surrender all, God wraps His arms of love around me, fills me with Himself, draws me near to His heart, and holds me close until I can hear His own heartbeat. The warmth of His love and the sweetness of His presence make everything else fade away. All I care about is Him. And provision is made.

....

....

....

....

....

....

....

....

....

....

....

....

....

....

Let us draw near to God with a sincere heart in full assurance of faith, having our hearts sprinkled to cleanse us from a guilty conscience.

HEBREWS 10:22

MOURN EVERYTHING
HOPEFULLY

For while we are in this tent, we groan and are burdened, because we do not wish to be unclothed but to be clothed with our heavenly dwelling.... Now it is God who has made us for this very purpose and has given us the Spirit as a deposit, guaranteeing what is to come.

2 CORINTHIANS 5:4–5

Sometimes I have to remind myself that our lives here are temporary. They are like the narthex to a grand cathedral. Several years ago I went to London's Westminster Abbey— the cathedral where kings and queens are crowned, where members of the royal family are married, and where dignitaries are buried. The door to the cathedral was small and insignificant, and once I walked through it, I entered another insignificant place: a dark, cramped narthex where I bought my ticket and guidebook.

On the opposite side of the narthex, another door led to the magnificent, cavernous sanctuary of the cathedral itself. I can't imagine anyone being satisfied with staying in the narthex of Westminster Abbey, clutching a ticket and studying the guidebook! The whole purpose of the narthex is to provide a place to get the ticket and make the transition into the cathedral itself.

Why do we cling so tightly to the narthex of this life? Why do we get our ticket to heaven, read the guidebook of God's Word, and then grieve and mourn at the thought of leaving the narthex and entering the extraordinary sanctuary of our Father's house?

When I've been tormented by guilt, I've found that I have to talk to God about the reasons for it. I have to get to the bottom of my feelings by confessing my sin specifically by name. I have to confess my failures and mistakes and shortcomings to Him. Would you do the same? Be specific. Ask God to forgive you. He promises He will. Then you must—it's not an option, you *must*—forgive yourself.

*Therefore...I want you to know that through Jesus
the forgiveness of sins is proclaimed to you.*

ACTS 13:38

As you examine your life—your daily, weekly, and monthly schedule; your priorities, activities, and goals—how much of it has eternal value? How much of the way you spend the majority of your time and attention and thoughts and money and energy will last beyond your lifetime?

Do not store up for yourselves treasures on earth, where moth and rust destroy, and where thieves break in and steal. But store up for yourselves treasures in heaven, where moth and rust do not destroy, and where thieves do not break in and steal.

MATTHEW 6:19-20

*D*eath has seemed to bring life more into focus for me. Has it done the same for you? If life is not about more than just living at the present, it's basically meaningless.

*I know that my Redeemer lives,
and that in the end he will stand upon the earth.
And...in my flesh I will see God.*

The apostle Paul said that the physical body of a child of God is like a tent. In other words, all that I am in my personality, emotions, will, and intellect—all of that which is "me"—lives inside the tent. When I die, I simply fold up my tent, but I continue to live more fully and abundantly than ever before!

Now we know that if the earthly tent we live in is destroyed, we have a building from God, an eternal house in heaven, not built by human hands.

2 CORINTHIANS 5:1

*P*raise God! One day we will have brand-new bodies! There are days when I can hardly wait.

*Listen, I tell you a mystery: We will not all sleep, but we will all be changed—
in a flash, in the twinkling of an eye, at the last trumpet. For the trumpet will
sound, the dead will be raised imperishable, and we will be changed.*

1 CORINTHIANS 15:51–52

*H*allelujah! Relief is coming! There is a new day—and a new body—on its way!

Our citizenship is in heaven. And we eagerly await a Savior from there, the Lord Jesus Christ, who, by the power that enables him to bring everything under his control, will transform our lowly bodies so that they will be like his glorious body.

*D*o you believe, with Job and Abraham and Martha and Paul, that in your flesh you will one day *see God*? And that you will one day see your family members and friends who had placed their faith in Him and who have already moved to the Father's house? I have answered yes. Yes! *YES! I believe!* Praise God for the living hope of the resurrection!

....

....

....

....

....

....

....

....

....

....

....

....

....

....

Praise be to the God and Father of our Lord Jesus Christ!
In his great mercy he has given us new birth into a living hope
through the resurrection of Jesus Christ from the dead.

1 PETER 1:3

PASS EVERYTHING ON

I have fought the good fight, I have finished the race, I have kept the faith. Now there is in store for me the crown of righteousness, which the Lord, the righteous Judge, will award to me on that day—and not only to me, but also to all who have longed for his appearing.

2 TIMOTHY 4:7–8

One of [my children's] favorite events is the relay race. As each race begins, the first runner from each team crouches at the starting block, gripping the baton in his hand. When the signal to begin is given, the runner explodes out of the starting block and runs the first leg of the race as swiftly as he can. In full stride, the first runner shifts the baton to his right hand, stretches out his arm, and, with his teammate running full speed alongside him, he passes the baton into the outstretched hand of the second runner. The second runner then runs his portion of the race and passes the baton to the number three runner, who also takes it in full stride, and so on until the last runner on the team crosses the finish line, tightly clutching the all-important baton.

Winning a relay race depends not only on the speed of the runners but also on their skillful ability to transfer the baton. If the baton is dropped, precious seconds are wasted, and the race may be lost. If the runner fails to pass the baton, he is disqualified from the race altogether.

The race of life is very similar to the relay race. The "baton" is the truth that leads to personal faith in God. Each person, or even each generation, that receives the baton runs the race to the best of his or her ability.

Will God bring about for me what He has promised because He knows I will direct my children to keep His ways? Think this through in application to your own life. What are you actively, intentionally doing to direct your children *after you* to keep the way of the Lord?

....

....

....

....

....

....

....

....

....

....

....

....

....

....

....

....

I have chosen him, so that he will direct his children and his household after him to keep the way of the LORD by doing what is right and just, so that the LORD will bring about for Abraham what he has promised him.

GENESIS 18:19

Who will pursue God because I do? And what about you? Who will make it the priority of their lives to know God as Abraham did, and make Him known to others, because you have? Who will refuse to settle for anything less than everything God wants to give them because you've refused to settle for less?

Let us hold unswervingly to the hope we profess, for he who promised is faithful. And let us consider how we may spur one another on toward love and good deeds.

HEBREWS 10:23-24

Through faith in His death and resurrection, we can be forgiven of our sin, be reconciled to the Father, and come back into the purpose for which we were originally created. But that sacrifice is effective only for those who claim it for themselves by faith. And how will anyone know to do that unless they are told?

*Consequently, faith comes from hearing the message,
and the message is heard through the word of Christ.*

If the people we tell are not interested—if they reject the Father's offer of His Son—then we are released from our obligation. We are not to force or coerce anyone to accept Jesus as his or her personal Savior and Lord. We just move on and tell someone else.

I have told you these things, so that in me you may have peace. In this world you will have trouble. But take heart! I have overcome the world.

As you and I go into all the world to seek those who would come into a love relationship with the Father's Son, the task is formidable. The world is a great big place, and the journey can be filled with hazardous dangers. How can we find those whose hearts are inclined to respond to the Father's invitation? Follow the servant's example. Before going out into your day, take a moment to pray first and ask God to lead you.

All authority in heaven and on earth has been given to me.
Therefore go and make disciples of all nations.... And surely I am
with you always, to the very end of the age.

MATTHEW 28:18-20

*G*od will lead you and me to those He has prepared to belong to His Son, just as He led Abraham's servant to Rebekah. One of the most exciting aspects of living a God-filled life has been to discover the "divine appointments" He places in my path.

....

....

....

....

....

....

....

....

....

....

....

....

....

....

....

....

....

....

....

....

....

....

....

....

....

....

....

....

....

If anyone speaks, he should do it as one speaking the very words of God.
If anyone serves, he should do it with the strength God provides,
so that in all things God may be praised through Jesus Christ.

1 PETER 4:11

What is keeping you so preoccupied that you don't open your eyes to the ones He places in your path? Why are you so afraid to open your mouth and say something? Are you trying to make it more complicated than it is? Is it because you are afraid of failure?

....

....

....

....

....

....

....

....

....

....

....

....

....

....

*We speak as men approved by God to be entrusted with the gospel.
We are not trying to please men but God, who tests our hearts.*

1 THESSALONIANS 2:4

*H*ave you lost contact with someone you have shared the gospel with? Just pray and ask God to reconnect you in some way. If He doesn't, then trust that He will send another one of His servants to make the offer again and bring it to a conclusion.

....

....

....

....

....

....

....

....

....

....

....

....

....

....

....

....

....

*Let us not become weary in doing good, for at the proper time
we will reap a harvest if we do not give up.*

GALATIANS 6:9

What has God done for you lately? What specific prayer has He answered? When have you told someone else about it in such a way that he or she could almost visualize His faithfulness to you?

....

....

....

....

....

....

....

....

....

....

....

....

....

....

....

....

....

....

....

....

....

....

....

*No eye has seen,
no ear has heard,
no mind has conceived
what God has prepared for those who love him.*

1 CORINTHIANS 2:9

*T*ell others that God so loves them that if they would choose to place their faith in His only beloved Son, Jesus, they would not perish in a life of separation from Him, but they would enter into a personal, permanent relationship with Him. Go ahead. Let them see the joy you feel as you tell them God's love story.

O LORD, you are my God; I will exalt you and praise your name, for in perfect faithfulness you have done marvelous things, things planned long ago.

ISAIAH 25:1

The "jewels" displayed in my life ought to make others want to know God as I do. Others ought to look at me and listen to me and want to love Jesus as I do. The magnificent obsession should be contagious simply by the way others see me embrace it for myself.

....

....

....

....

....

....

....

....

....

....

....

....

....

....

Now to him who is able to do immeasurably more than all we ask or imagine, according to his power that is at work within us, to him be glory in the church and in Christ Jesus throughout all generations, for ever and ever! Amen.

EPHESIANS 3:20–21

My father passed on to me an authentic, God-filled life by his example as well as his preaching. My father and my mother both embraced the magnificent obsession of knowing God and making Him known...and it has become my own. I now have the privilege of passing it on...*to you*!

....

....

....

....

....

....

....

....

....

....

....

....

....

....

....

Do not forget the things your eyes have seen or let them slip from your heart as long as you live. Teach them to your children and to their children after them.

ow it's your turn. Don't drop the baton! Once you have embraced the magnificent obsession for yourself...once you have embraced a truly God-filled life, pass everything on until your faith becomes sight and you see the only beloved Son of the Father face-to-face. On that day, you are going to see His desire for you as though you're the only one He loves.

*The Father himself loves you because you have loved me
and have believed that I came from God.*

JOHN 16:27

*P*raise God! Praise God! He has promised that these "jewels" are just the down payment [on His gifts to come]:

- His joy that is unspeakable and full of glory. (See 1 Peter 1:8.)

- His peace that passes all understanding. (See Philippians 4:7.)

- His love that will not let me go. (See Romans 8:38–39.)

- His compassion that never fails. (See Lamentations 3:22.)

- His forgiveness of every sin and all sin. (See 1 John 1:7, 9.)

- His life that is abundant and free. (See John 10:10.)

- His blessings that are unlimited. (See John 1:16.)

- His mercy in my failure. (See 1 Timothy 1:16.)

- His strength that is made perfect in my weakness. (See 2 Corinthians 12:9.)

- His grace that is sufficient for my every need. (See 2 Corinthians 12:9; Ephesians 1:6.)

- His family that surrounds me with support and encouragement. (See Ephesians 1:18.)

- His Word that is so personal and powerful and true. (See 2 Timothy 3:16–17.)

- His faithfulness that continues to all generations. (See Psalm 119:90.)

- His Spirit that will never leave me nor forsake me. (See John 14:16.)

- And the blessed hope of one day seeing Him face-to-face! (See Titus 2:13; Revelation 22:4.)

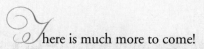
There is much more to come!

Ellie Claire™ Gift & Paper Corp.
Minneapolis, MN 55438
www.ellieclaire.com

EMBRACING GOD
Journal
© 2010 by Anne Graham Lotz

ISBN 978-1-60936-015-3

Compiled by Marilyn Jansen
Cover and interior design by Lisa and Jeff Franke.

Printed in China.